Needlework Treasures from the Orient

Marsha McKerr

VNR Van Nostrand Reinhold Company

For

Joan Toggitt and Elizabeth P. Burroughs,
and especially, Jason McKerr, Megan
McKerr, and Richard McKerr

Copyright © 1984 by Van Nostrand Reinhold Company
 Inc.
Library of Congress Catalog Card Number 84-7331
ISBN 0-442-24435-5

Printed in the United States of America

Designed by Ginger Legato

Published by Van Nostrand Reinhold Company Inc.
135 West 50th Street
New York, New York 10020

Van Nostrand Reinhold Company Limited
Molly Millars Lane
Wokingham, Berkshire RG11 2PY, England

Van Nostrand Reinhold
480 La Trobe Street
Melbourne, Victoria 3000, Australia

Macmillan of Canada
Division of Gage Publishing Limited
164 Commander Boulevard
Agincourt, Ontario M1S 3C7, Canada

16 15 14 13 12 11 10 9 8 7 6 5 4 3 2 1

Library of Congress Cataloging in Publication Data

McKerr, Marsha.
    Needlework treasures from the Orient.

    Bibliography: p.
    Includes index.
    1. Needlework—Patterns. I. Title.
TT753.M38 1984   746.44   84-7331
ISBN 0-442-24435-5

Contents

A great many people and organizations have given invaluable assistance since the beginning of the long process that led to this book. I would like particularly to thank Megan, Jason, and Richard McKerr for their gracious understanding and tolerance; Donna McTiernan for meticulous care and patience in charting; Susan Smith, Edie Fisher, and Karin Lidbeck for all their efforts and hard work during the photography sessions, for the stitch diagrams, for helping to organize me, and for helping my spelling.

Thanks also to: Piri Palmai for her innovative and careful finishing and sewing skills; Michigo Bosuego; Peter Orkin for his photographs; Mitsuhiro Abe and Jean Mailey of the Metropolitan Museum of Art; Professor Wong Sui-Ling; The China Institute; Boston Museum of Fine Arts; Jenny So of the Fogg Museum; Yen Cheng Institute; China Trade Museum; Peter and Louise Rosenberg of the Vallin Gallery; Bob Winston of the Tulip Tree Gallery; Ann Wolff of Rare Art, Inc.; Jonathan Kimpel of Kimpel Display; and Nancy Green and Susan Gies for their editing and extreme patience.

Introduction

The artistic skill of the Chinese has led to the creation of some of the finest porcelain, painting, poetry, embroidery, jade work, and fabric in all the world. These art forms have been treated with respect and subsidized by attitude, custom, and, to varying degrees, emperors and their governments. They are an inherent part of the people's lives—their history, folklore, religion, philosophy, and language—and are both an expression and a vehicle for expression.

In all of the various arts there exists a pattern of culture woven with the threads of a "symbolic alphabet" spun from the fibers of tradition. The direct origins of most of the symbols inherent in the designs and motifs are lost in the four-thousand-year-old mists of antiquity. There was an ancient universal theory developed and used to explain all natural phenomena. This theory was called "The Five Elements." The Five Elements—Earth, Wood, Fire, Metal, and Water—together with the Yin and Yang principle of cosmic harmony—positive and negative interaction, darkness and light, male and female, heaven and earth—were used for the development of a system of classification and symbolic correlations for every particle of the universe. This system was liberally sprinkled with legends and myths of demons and fairies, gods and princesses, dragons, and even a Chinese Cinderella—all laden with morals designed to direct behavior and attitudes.

Crowning all of this is the ancient custom of ancestor worship and the binding loyalty of the family. This patriarchal theme was important and pervasive. The souls of ancestors demanded constant attention, and this naturally led to the desire for a great number of children; for in children lay perpetuity and immortality. This reverence for antiquity and ancestral custom was extended to the repeated use of designs and motifs that have been elaborated and stylized into a constant and continuous thread throughout Chinese history to the present day.

Another vastly important fiber running throughout China's arts is the use of the *rebus* (a form of riddle created by expressing a word or an attitude by using a picture of an object whose name resembles the word or attitude) and the *homonym* (a word that is pronounced the same as another word but that has a different meaning). The Chinese language, both written and spoken, lends itself quite naturally to these. The rebus and the homonym have been called the "shadow language" of Chinese symbolism, as certain words in Chinese are pronounced exactly like the written character for a totally different word. An example of this visual pun is the vase in the Spring Vase Hanging (page 29) and in the Manchurian Crane Pillow (page 66). The word for vase, *"p'ing,"* is a homonym for the word for tranquillity. The rebus is created by portraying the vase as a major or minor part of a design to express the desire for peace and tranquillity. Some symbols can be translated quite literally and directly, while others represent an ideal or a particular notion. These idea associations are a concrete means of expressing a living tradition and the essence of aesthetic ideals.

The binding loyalty of the family and the use of metaphoric language and inherent symbolism was augmented by the introduction of philosophical and religious beliefs, specifically, Confucianism, Taoism, and Buddhism. These varied religions and philosophies, which were introduced in China at different times, were accepted, assimilated, and then intricately interwoven into a network of attitudes and ideas that furnished the arts with a superlative abundance of decorative motifs.

The expression of harmony between man and nature is a basic and constant theme running throughout Chinese tradition and art. Eastern man sees himself as a harmonious part of the natural world and seems to convey an intimacy with it and an understanding of it. Birds, flowers, and rocks (for even rocks have souls) are portrayed with dignity and beauty, demonstrating their embodiment of life and spirit.

The symbolism is all-encompassing and, although it may be "mysterious," it is explicable. However, a hundred or so explanations or nuances may be needed for each motif or combination of motifs. The repeated use of symbolism should be considered as an extension of the desire for per-petuity, of the reverence for antiquity and cultural tradition. While this culture of classical traditions has absorbed and assimilated outside influences from time to time, it has changed, developed, and re-freshed itself—yet it manages to maintain its original base. All the symbols used in the visual portrayal of abstract ideals are beneficent: the symbols bear no evil intent but consistently express the Five Blessings—Happiness, Wealth and Honors, Tran-quillity, Virtue, Long and Pleasing Life. The Chinese language, legends, philosophies, and religions, en-twined with simple hopes and dreams, are wrapped in strictly prescribed codes of behavior, ethics, and mores; they are tightly tied with the ribbons of tradition and custom.

Sometimes a piece is so pleasing to the eye in its mellifluous composition of color and line, or it is so appealing in its vibrant qualities, that its metaphoric language goes unnoticed. Of course, it is not necessary to understand the origins and the meanings of the symbols or the metaphoric language to be able to appreciate the composition, integrity, and charm of a design. Nevertheless, as Alan Priest remarks in *Costumes from the Forbidden City,* "there remains the whispered persistence of things learned long, long ago—before memory—which, though expressed are unspoken, though felt are not tangible."

About Needlework

As an art, needlework has survived many social trends, and, although the needle arts are no longer a requirement for the "proper upbringing of young ladies," today millions of people, both men and women, enjoy them. Perhaps needlework is a sanctuary from our highly mechanized society. It is something that computers cannot do and, even if they could, the result could never be as special as the work you have done yourself.

The terms *needlework* and *needle arts* incorporate many techniques—needlepoint, cross-stitch, embroidery, appliqué, and quilting, among others. The designs in this book have been rendered either in needlepoint or in counted cross-stitch. Any of the sixteen designs or four additional designs can be done in either technique.

When you choose to do a piece, use only the best materials available. In addition to making your work easier, they will help to make your finished piece more elegant, valuable, and ultimately more beautiful.

Tools and Materials

Having the proper tools and materials will also make your project easier.

Scissors. Embroidery scissors are nice to have, but they are not absolutely necessary. It is only important that your scissors be sharp and manageable. (Kitchen shears are not.)

Needles. Tapestry needles, which are used for cross-stitch and needlepoint, have a dull point and a large eye. They come in many sizes and are easily obtainable. Use a small needle for fine mesh canvas and even-weave fabric and, correspondingly, a larger one for canvases and fabrics with a larger mesh.

Thimble. Some people use thimbles, others do not. I use one for needlepoint, but I do not use one for cross-stitch. If you use a thimble, make sure that it is comfortable or you will defeat the purpose of using it.

Canvas. There are two basic types of canvas, mono and penelope. Mono canvas is a weave of single threads in each direction, and penelope is a weave of double threads in each direction. Mono canvas is the more commonly used of the two today.

Both types of canvas come in different mesh sizes. The mesh size is the number of stitches per inch (that is, #14 canvas means 14 stitches per inch). The lower the number of stitches, the coarser the canvas.

Canvas is usually sold by the yard. There are a number of widths and grades of canvas quality. Be certain of the finished size of your project and allow adequate margins (usually 2 inches—5 cm—beyond the stitched area on each side) before purchasing your canvas. The best quality of canvas will give the best results for stitching and finishing.

Even the best canvas can have a knot in the weave from time to time, so check carefully to be sure that there will be no knots in your stitching area.

Even-Weave Fabrics. There are many different kinds and colors of even-weave fabrics. Again, the lower the mesh size, the coarser the fabric; fewer stitches are required to cover an area. There are many different types of weaves—and each offers a different textural effect. These different weaves, such as Aida, Davos, Linda, etc., can be found in needlecraft shops. The warp and weft threads are consistent and easy to count so that the placement of stitches is obvious. There are also a vast number of colors available in the different weaves. The color of the fabric and the type of weave are both very important considerations when purchasing fabric for a project since they are not covered by stitches.

Again, buy only the best quality for the best results and check carefully for knots or flaws.

Frames and Hoops. Frames and hoops are more a matter of preference than a requirement. I prefer to work needlepoint without a frame, and a small project in cross-stitch is easier for me to work without a hoop. However, I prefer to handle a large project in cross-stitch on a large hoop or a frame.

Yarns. There are many different types of yarn. The primary consideration should be to use a yarn that evenly covers the canvas or fabric. If a yarn is too fine, the canvas or background material will show through the stitches. If a yarn is too heavy, it will pull the fabric out of shape drastically, and the result will be lumpy, not smooth as it should be.

Use only yarns that are made specifically for needlework. Other types—knitting yarn, for example—are not designed to hold up to the repeated wear of being pulled through the canvas or fabric, of being blocked, and of the long-term use expected of the finished piece.

Again, quality is of the utmost importance whether you are using wool, silk, cotton, or linen.

Working with the Charts

Each square on the charts in this book represents one needlework stitch. The symbol indicates the color used. A color key accompanies the chart. Naturally, the charts are of varying sizes, depending on the design. Please note the stitch counts carefully. The finished size of your piece will depend on the fabric or canvas weave. For example, if the stitch count of the charted design is 40 by 40 stitches, the stitched design area will be:

on 10-count fabric	4 by 4 inches (10 by 10cm)
on 14-count fabric	2.8 by 2.8 inches (7 by 7cm)
on 18-count fabric	2.25 by 2.25 inches (5.6 by 5.6cm)
on 22-count fabric	1.8 by 1.8 inches (4.5 by 4.5cm)

The colors used in the projects are matched as closely as possible to the original researched pieces. All of these colors are referred to by name and also by DMC cotton floss numbers or Paternayan Persian wool numbers so you may accurately reproduce the shading if you so choose. DMC and Paternayan color cards are readily available in most needlework shops. Refer to them if you want to match them to colors of different yarns. Color schemes may be easily altered to suit a project or decor. Experiment with your own colors to create an individual project.

Stitches

The basic stitches for both needlepoint and cross-stitch are quite simple and easy to do. There are a multitude of beautiful and effective stitches that may interest you, but you need only a few to work the projects in this book. You can work the designs in the needlepoint tent stitch, or you may choose to work any design in counted cross-stitch. If you prefer more elaborate stitches, refer to some of the excellent needlework books on the market for help. In some designs, different stitches have been used for effect. These have been indicated and stitch diagrams accompany the individual charts. Here, too, you have the option of using the stitches shown or choosing the basic stitches. Again, you may decide on any stitch depending on the effect you are aiming for.

Needlepoint. Needlepoint encompasses a great variety and number of stitches, all of which are developed from the two basic stitches; the diagonal or tent stitch and the straight stitch or Gobelin. The tent stitch is a diagonal stitch that extends from the lower left to upper right covering one intersection of horizontal and vertical threads. It is the most commonly used stitch and has several different names depending on the method in which it is worked.

The Continental tent stitch is used when working a single row of tent stitches horizontally, vertically, or diagonally. (Fig. 1: Bring needle up at odd numbers, down at even.) It should be used for working design areas and border patterns but not for backgrounds, as it tends to pull the canvas out of shape.

Note: one square on a chart represents one tent stitch.

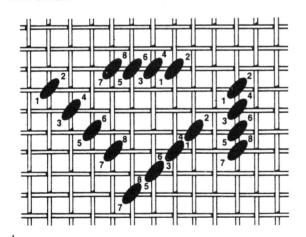

1
The Continental method for tent stitch. Bring needle up at 1, down at 2, up at 3, etc.

The basketweave method of the tent stitch is used when working an area with several rows of stitches. (Fig. 2: Bring needle up at odd numbers, down at even.) It is worked diagonally. When the basketweave stitch is worked, the wrong side of

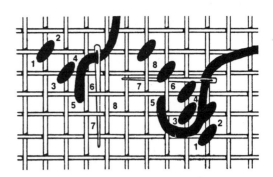

2
The basketweave method for tent stitch.

the work looks like a "basket weave," and the finished project will be very smooth and even.

Cross-Stitch. Counted cross-stitch is simply working one cross-stitch to correspond to each square on the design chart, counting the corresponding squares and stitches as the design is applied to the fabric. You may complete each stitch as you work. (Fig. 3: Bring needle up at odd numbers, down at even. Fig. 4: Alternate method, work the stitches in two journeys.)

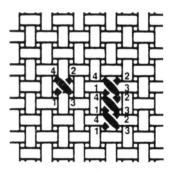

3
Cross-stitches worked individually.

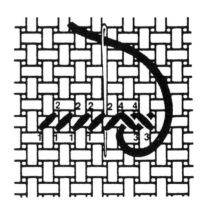

4
Cross-stitches worked in two journeys.

Outline Detail. Outline detail (indicated by dark lines on the charts) may be worked by back-stitching (Fig. 5) *after* the needlepoint or cross-stitch design has been completed.

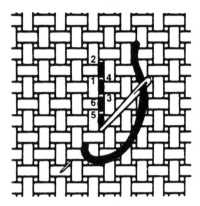

5
Backstitching is used as outline detail.

Stitching Tips

Following these steps will help you avoid problems in stitching and finishing.

- Always allow adequate margins beyond the working area (approximately 2 inches—5 cm—on each side) to accommodate the appropriate finishing technique.
- Bind the raw edges of canvas with masking tape or stitch bias tape to raw edges. For even-weave and other fabrics, simply overcast the raw edges.
- Locate and mark the horizontal and vertical centers of the canvas with thread. This is easily done by folding the canvas in half horizontally and then basting along the fold. Repeat the process vertically.
- Start your work in the center, where your basting stitches meet.
- When working with stranded yarn or thread, separate the strands and realign them before you thread your needle. Check the "grain" of the yarn and thread the needle with the end that leads the smoothest journey.
- To anchor your yarn when starting, bring your needle through your first stitch opening from the back to the front of your fabric, leaving about an inch of yarn on the back. Hold this tail of yarn on the back and catch it with the first four or five stitches so that it is secure. *Never* use a knot to begin or end your yarn. It will create lumps and can come untied.
- Once your work is in progress, a new strand of yarn should be anchored by weaving the new yarn in and out of several stitches on the back of the fabric or by catching the tail with the first few stitches. To end a strand of yarn, you should again weave it in and out of several stitches on the back side of your fabric. Again, do not use a knot. Trim the excess yarn after weaving the ends securely.
- Keep your stitching tension as consistent as possible, bearing in mind that if you pull stitches too tight, the fabric will pucker or pull the work out of shape. If you have difficulty in keeping your stitches consistent, a frame or hoop will be a great help.

Finishing

There are three basic steps in finishing needlework: check the piece, wash (when necessary) and block the piece, and mount the piece.

Checking the Work. To check your needlework, first make sure you have covered all pattern areas. Then examine the back side of the work to make sure that all yarn ends are anchored securely. Trim any excess ends.

Washing. You need not wash a piece of needlework unless it has become soiled while you worked the piece.

Before washing any piece of needlework, make sure that your thread is colorfast. Both needlepoint and cross-stitch should be washed by hand. Use cool water and very gentle soap. Rinse the piece well. Do *not* wring out the excess water. Roll the piece inside of a towel and squeeze to eliminate the excess water, then block.

Blocking. Blocking is the process of straightening needlework so the threads of the canvas are again horizontally and vertically true.

As cross-stitch does not tend to pull the fabric out of shape, a light pressing is usually all that is required. Use a damp pressing cloth on the wrong side of the work and press gently. If you have washed your cross-stitch piece, place it face down on a towel and, using a pressing cloth, iron it dry.

If major areas of a needlework piece have been worked in the Continental tent stitch instead of the basketweave tent stitch, the piece may require blocking several times before you get it squared.

A needlepoint piece that was not washed should be dampened by going over the wrong side of the embroidery with a wet sponge. Then straighten and fasten the canvas to a blocking board. Use rustproof push-pins and align the weave as you pull the canvas taut. Allow the canvas to dry quite thoroughly, at least a day, before removing it from the blocking board.

Mounting

As I am not a professional seamstress or picture framer, I feel strongly that the work into which I put great time and effort should be finished by those who do finishing professionally. Many local needlework shops have marvelous people who do different kinds of mounting with great skill. Upholsterers and decorators are also great sources for pillow finishing, coordinating fabrics, and clever finishing touches. Frame shops have the proper tools and equipment to do the job well and give your piece the attention it deserves. If you are one of those fortunate, clever people who has the skills to mount your own work, there are very good books available that are filled with finishing ideas and instructions.

Sixteen Designs

The following designs have been chosen from many different sources, from paintings and elegant jade carvings to "simple" folk art prints and fabulous silk embroideries. Historical information and notes accompany each of the designs that have been used to create pillows, hangings, panels, a rug, and pictures. The designs can be adapted to many uses to suit your needs and taste.

Ming Bird Panel

The *k'o-ssu* panel from which this piece was adapted is part of the textile collection at the Metropolitan Museum of Art. It is believed to date back to the Ming dynasty (1368–1644). The style of the piece is quite unusual for a Chinese tapestry; it is actually more reminiscent of porcelain decoration in the distinctive cloud patterns that echo the styles of blue and white porcelain decorations of the fifteenth and sixteenth centuries.

The word *k'o-ssu* is the transliteration of Chinese characters that mean "cut silk," "crossed threads," "carved silk," and "weft-woven colors." *K'o-ssu* is a special type of silk weaving that allowed great freedom in the creation of the design and the desired effects and, therefore, allowed the re-creation of painted porcelain decoration.

The design is composed of various birds, flowers, and distinctive scalloped clouds—all of which carry their own symbolic meanings. The birds include a magpie, a kingfisher, a falcon, a sparrow, and what seems to be a nightingale. Although the flowers in the lower part of the panel appear to be exotics,

the traditional snowball and the flowering plum are evident in the upper part. The clouds, which are the symbol of heaven and the bearers of life-giving rain, are effective both as a symbol and as a complement to the symphony of birds and flowers. They seem to augment the spirit of life and movement inherent in the piece.

Some of the birds are clearly fantastic fabrications; others, while realistic looking, are not in any of Audubon's work. Some were chosen for their symbolic implications; others were used for their color or lineal form or perhaps simply for the expression of an attitude, such as the freedom expressed in the flight of a bird.

The magpie, or "lucky bird" (upper portion, far left, with wings spread), is regarded as a bird of good omen, even though it is considered to be given to flattery. The Chinese character for magpie translates literally as "bird of joy," and its voice is said to impart encouragement to the hearer. Even though the kingfisher (lower portion, right side) is also considered vain—because its magnificent blue-green plumage is thought to "rival the sky and the far distant hills"—it is regarded as a special emblem of beauty. Its feathers were highly prized for their beauty and were used as motifs in needlework, jewelry, and ornament.

The mighty falcon (large bird in center) is emblematic of boldness and keen vision, of courage, power, and heroism, not only because the bird is possessed of these qualities, but also because its name, *ying*, is a homonym for the word "heroic." In contrast to the mighty falcon is the little sparrow, which, although small and less dramatic, is highly esteemed as a symbol of loyalty and of promises kept. The nightingale (upper portion, center, perched on the branch) is a herald of spring, as it begins its magnificent song in February, the end of winter and the beginning of the new year. Even though the nightingale seems to be the antithesis of the kingfisher and the magpie, its song and its seasonal arrival make it emblematic of beauty and joy. As this little bird's plumage is so drab and colorless, it is more often "heard" in poetry and legend than seen in the pictorial arts.

The plum blossom, bringing with it the promise of spring and the renewal of hope, is also highly prized for its fragrance, snowy purity, and beauty. It also denotes courage, as it is the first blossom to brave the frosts of winter. The snowball, a type of chrysanthemum, is a popular design motif. It was also a favorite of the Dowager Empress, Tz'u Hsi, who raised the flower. Perhaps she enjoyed snowballs because they were believed to possess "magic juices," as well as beauty. This great lady ate the petals of the flower after they had been dipped in alum and dropped into boiling chicken soup. The snowball is a symbol of gaiety, fidelity, and courage, as it outlasts the first frosts of winter. Because it also signifies long duration, it is emblematic of mature happiness and leisure.

The cloud and thunder line, or connected T pattern border, implies happiness and well wishes, as it is an emblem of good fortune and continued prosperity.

The entire panel is an orchestration of theme and countertheme, color, lineal form, custom, and beauty. It bears the wish that "courage, joy, and loyalty—along with a beauty as magnificent as spring and the freedom of the birds—be of long and lasting duration."

Ming Bird Panel		DMC Colors
∴	Ecru	—
∧	Light Beige	842
◆	Beige	841
✕	Brown	433
＼	Light Rust	945
✖	Rust	356
■	Black	310
○	Light Green	504
▲	Medium Green	502
∨	Dark Green	924
⊃	Light Blue	775
△	Medium Blue	932
●	Dark Blue	930
✛	Blue Black	336
∪	Gray	648

Stitch Count: 210 by 507

Ming Bird Panel

Ming Bird: Upper left

Ming Bird: Upper right

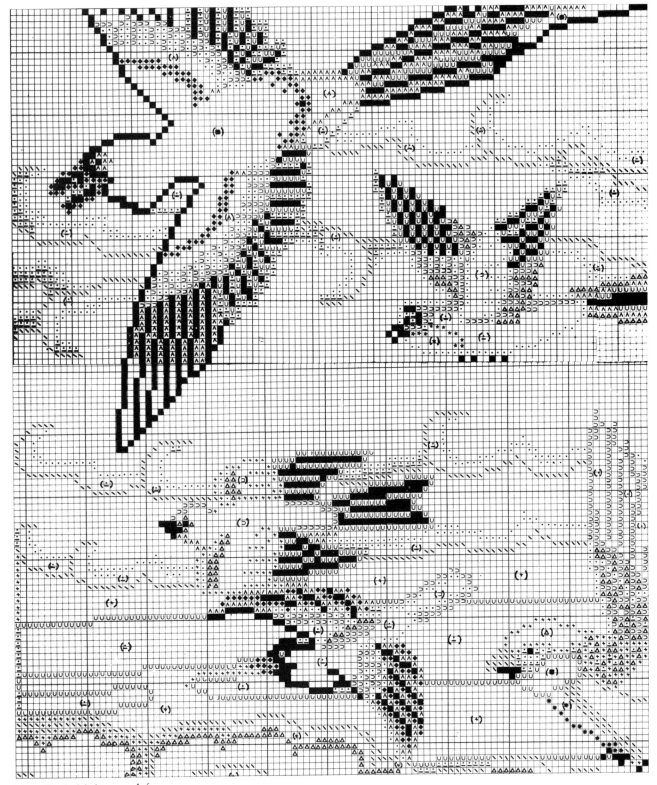

Ming Bird: Mid-upper left

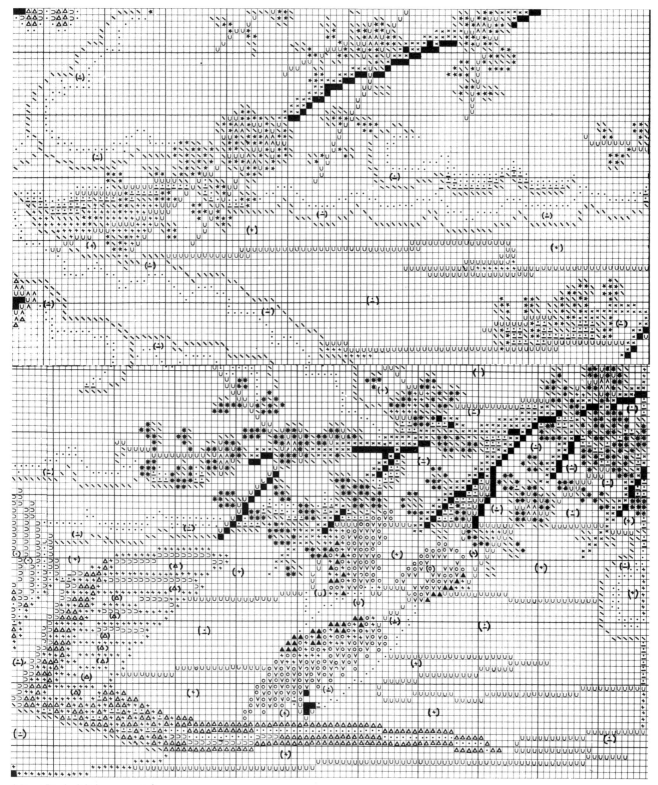

Ming Bird: Mid-upper right

Ming Bird: Mid-lower left

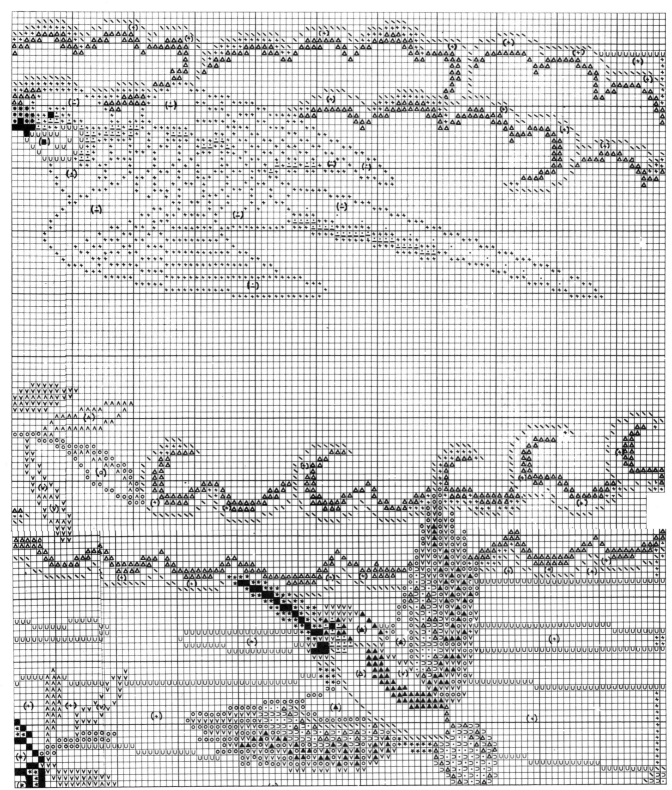

Ming Bird: Mid-lower right

Ming Bird: Lower left

Ming Bird: Lower right

Narcissus and *Shou* Rug

The narcissus and *shou* pattern is taken from an informal *k'o-ssu* court robe believed to have belonged to the Dowager Empress Tz'u Hsi (1835–1908) of the Ch'ing dynasty. Her love for beautiful clothes was second only to her consuming passsion for ruling the country, which she did by the sheer force of her personality, keen mind, tireless energy, and devastating charm for forty-seven nearly undisputed years. She particularly disliked her formal imperial court robes, claiming that their yellow color made her look sallow. She subsequently had many robes designed to suit her own refined and genteel tastes. Of the thousands she is said to have possessed, one striking characteristic is the frequently used motif of naturalistic floral sprays. The narcissus—bulbs, roots, and all—was one of her particular favorites.

The word for narcissus, *shui hsien*, means "water fairy" and is a symbol of immortality and good omen. It is variously cited as the winter flower and the spring flower. It is generally cultivated and forced to bloom on New Year's Day, as it is regarded as a good omen for the coming year.

The large round *shou*, with the Oriental fylfot and the *hsi* incorporated and worked in diagonal patterns among the flowers, is another of the Dowager Empress's favorite motifs. It was prominent in many of her robes, and she did not permit others of the court to wear it.

The *shou* is an ideograph that, no matter in which of its many forms it is given, means longevity. The fylfot is an ancient symbol for rolling thunder. It is also the short form of the character *wan*, which means "ten-thousand-fold" or "myriad," and is a symbol for happiness. The character *hsi* (in the center of the *shou* motif) means "joy" or "blessing." This form of the *shou*, therefore, becomes a very compact statement of the wish for "a very long and prosperous life blessed ten-thousand-fold by joy and happiness." Add to this the narcissus with its wish for the "continued beauty and promise of many springs yet to come." The red of the background adds a little joy and some virtue for good measure.

The butterfly (in the corners) is a symbol of beauty. The word for butterfly is *hu-tieh; hu* means

Narcissus and *Shou* Rug

20

"happiness," and *tieh* means "seventy to eighty years." So a butterfly as a design element is a rebus used to express the wish for "beauty and happiness in old age."

The outside border is an interlocking lineal T pattern with the fylfot and the cash, or coin, motif incorporated to express constant good fortune, complete harmony, and endless prosperity. The T pattern (or cloud and thunder pattern) is often used in varied forms, as shown in the border on the Ming Bird Panel. The cash motif represents the wish for "prosperity and riches" and represents the harmonious balance between heaven and earth.

Note: The pattern shown on the following pages is for the upper left quadrant of the rug only Because pattern is a repeat, you can simply work it backwards for the remaining quadrants (see photo in color section for complete rug).

Narcissus and *Shou* Rug		Paternayan
⚥	Lightest Green	354
∩	Light Green	532
−	Green	530
>	Dark Green	507
×	Light Gold	467
▲	Gold	445
○	White	005
/	Light Blue	396
△	Medium Blue	386
●	Blue	330
∨	Dark Blue	365
✝	Gold Metallic	—
◆	Red	240

Stitch Count (entire rug): 426 by 636

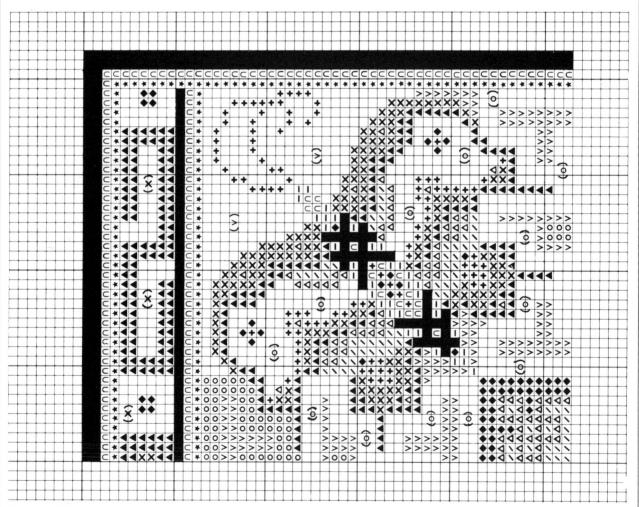

Upper lefthand corner of rug

Narcissus and *Shou*: Upper left

Narcissus and *Shou*: Lower left

Narcissus and *Shou*: Upper middle

Narcissus and *Shou*: Lower middle

26

Narcissus and *Shou*: Upper right

Narcissus and *Shou*: Lower right

Tiger Lilies Pillow (left)
Butterfly Pillow (right)
Center front: Original "Butterfly," embroidered with
silk threads and gold couching on silk. (Courtesy
of the Vallin Gallery)

Malay Peacock Pillow

Narcissus and Shou Rug (background)
Spring Vase Hanging
Narcissus and Hsi Evening Clutch
Manchurian Crane Pillow
Ming Basket Cushion

Ming Bird Panel

Lotus and Kingfisher Panel

Butterfly Scroll (left)
Spring Vase (right)

Narcissus and Shou Rug

Dragon-Fish Screen (top right)
Pomegranate and Butterfly Framed Picture (lower right)
Happy Augury Picture Set (left and center front)

Spring Vase Hanging

The original silk tapestry from which this piece is adapted is part of the collection of the National Palace Museum of Taipei, Taiwan. This silk hanging scroll is a reworking of an original painting by a Ch'ing dynasty emperor of the Ch'ien-lung period (1736–1795). The weaving is of remarkable skill, perhaps because it was a copy of the emperor's painting or perhaps because it was a copy of a remarkable piece. Copying was done not for the purpose of deception, but for veneration and perpetuity.

The piece is entitled *Symbols of Fulfillment of One's Wishes at the Beginning of Spring*. The wish expressed in the title is explicitly and far more elegantly expressed by the combination of the symbolic design motifs.

Pao p'ing, the rare vase, is a rebus for the "maintenance of peace" and therefore is a symbol of the desire for perpetual harmony and completeness. Arranged in the vase is a sprig of evergreen, a branch of plum or prunus blossoms, and colorful blossoms that may be peach or mallow blossoms.

The Chinese word for evergreen translates literally as "ten thousand years." Since the evergreen remains unchanged through all the seasons and lives to a great age, it is a symbol of constancy and friends who remain faithful in adversity. The evergreen held a place of honor in the emperor's gardens because of its attributes: constancy, age, and therefore, wisdom. The prunus blossoms—which appear in the last cold of winter—bear the promise of spring, beauty, courage, and the renewal of hope.

The red- and salmon-colored flowers look like mallow flowers, the emblem of the Lord of the Four Seasons. However, they might be peach blossoms, another emblem of spring and treasured as the fruit of life. The peach blossom represents youth and freshness and is used as a charm to ward off evil. Whichever flower was originally intended, the beauty and the intrinsic statement remain the same.

The persimmon, because of its warm red color, is a token of joy; the lily is a symbol for maternity and is used as a charm for dispelling grief. Together, the persimmon and lily represent creative power.

The cultivation of the sacred fungus in the footed bowl is the expression of the granting of every good wish or desire through the magical powers it is believed to possess.

The piece as a whole is a statement of completeness and perpetual harmony, of faithful friends, the constant renewal of hope, of freshness, joy, and inventiveness throughout a long and happy life—the "Fulfillment of One's Wishes at the Beginning of Spring."

	Spring Vase Hanging	DMC Colors
O	Dark Green	319
S	Light Brown	738
÷	Brown	801
v	Gray	318
x	White	—
△	Light Red	349
\	Medium Red	352
⊂	Pink	754
8	Yellow	676
◆	Dark Gray	317
U	Blue	336
▲	Medium Green	320
+	Pale Gray	762
■	Dark Red	817
☆	Gold Metallic	—
•	Light Green	369

Stitch Count: 133 by 232

Spring Vase Hanging

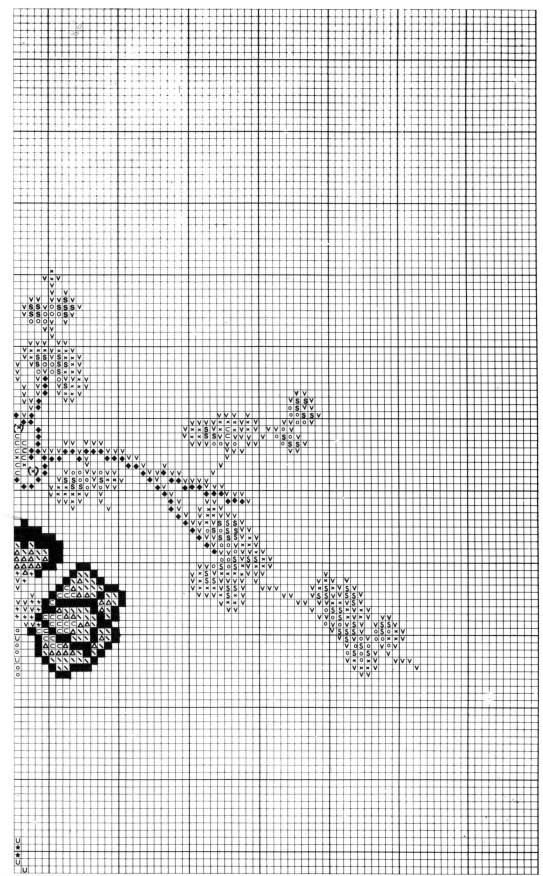

Spring Vase: Upper right

Spring Vase: Upper left

Spring Vase: Lower right

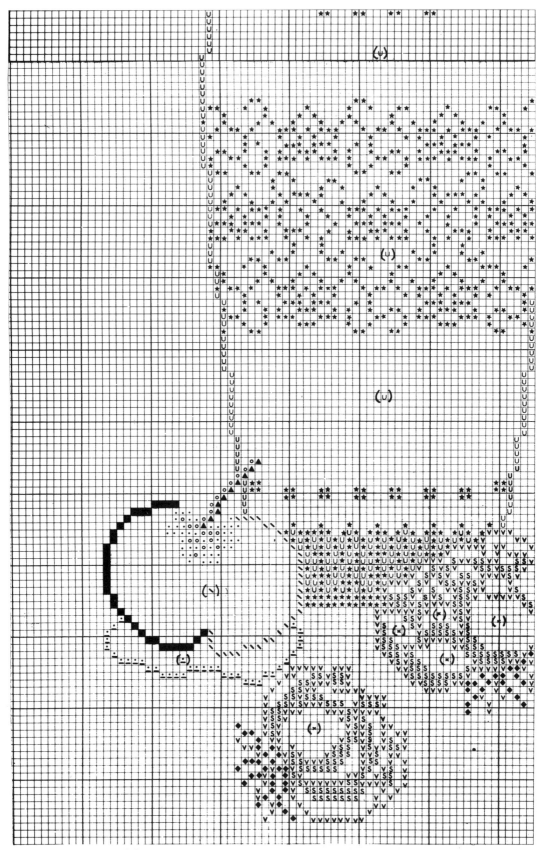

Spring Vase: Lower left

✍️ Dragon-Fish Screen

The original embroidery from which this was adapted is of the late-eigtheenth-century Ch'ing dynasty (1644–1911) and is now a part of the collection of the Metropolitan Museum of Art. Perhaps it was a graduation present from father to son, as it would have been worn by a scholar who had passed his examinations with the highest honors. The dragon-fish symbolizes a scholar of great perseverance and virtue.

The Chinese educational system was very demanding and was the only means of attaining high office, social position, honors, and recognition. It was believed that the carp—symbol of abundance and freedom—could ascend the rapids, succeed in passing through the Gate of Heaven, and become transformed into a dragon. This metamorphosis was considered analogous to the scholar's passing his examinations with distinction. The dragon, a most benevolent creature for the Chinese, is the essence of all natural forces and is free of all obstructions and restraints, just as the mind of the scholar is free and powerful.

Dragon-Fish Screen		DMC Colors
▲	Dark Blue	824
＼	Medium Blue	826
•	Light Blue	827
○	Red	817
＋	Yellow	729
■	Brown	801
＜	Dark Green	890
∩	Medium Green	502
△	Light Green	504
✗	Gold Metallic	—
-	Ecru	—
✷	Black	310

Stitch Count: 164 by 159

Dragon-Fish Screen

Dragon-Fish:
Left half

Dragon-Fish:
Right half

✌ Butterfly Scroll Plate Pillow

This design is not a direct adaptation of a specific piece, but rather a combination of the basic design motifs and ideas expressed in an eighteenth-century *famille rose* plate from the Ch'ing dynasty, the period when the porcelains began to show European influence.

The scroll, a symbol of learning and a charm against loneliness and evil spirits, is one of the four symbols of "Gentlemanly Accomplishments." The four Accomplishments and the use of their symbols reconfirm the importance of learning, culture, and social graces. The scroll was the means of preserving precious paintings and writings—the "Store of Truth"—and was used as the emblem of Han Shan's (a seventh-century poet) unfinished book on nature.

The butterflies' flight across the scroll, as it is unrolled, represents freedom, the freedom and power of the scholar's mind through his learning. Butterflies are representative of beauty, joy, and grace and excite emotions of delight.

The butterflies and the flowers on the open scrolls could also be construed as a simple statement of the Chinese artists' intrinsic love and respect for nature.

The chrysanthemum, in a highly convention-alized form, is scattered about the surface of the plate. As this beautiful flower of autumn outlasts the first frosts of winter, it is a symbol of fidelity and courage, of "consideration of long duration." It also suggests mature happiness and continued good cheer.

The Eternal Knot, or Mystic Knot of Everlasting Happiness (forming each of the four corners), is said to receive and forward abundance, and it symbolizes constant happiness and longevity.

Note: Only part of the border, which should extend all the way around , is shown in the following patterns. Continue border all the way around in same pattern (see photo in color section for complete border).

Butterfly Scroll Plate Pillow		DMC Colors
▲	Dark Blue	311
○	Light Blue	775
●	Dark Green	367
＼	Light Green	504
▰	Red	347
＋	Light Pink	818
∨	Pink	760
∧	Yellow	676
✕	Gray	318
⸫	Brown	433
＜	Medium Blue	932
✷	Gold	—

Stitch Count: 222 by 222

Butterfly Scroll Plate Pillow

Butterfly Scroll Plate: Upper left

Butterfly Scroll Plate: Upper right

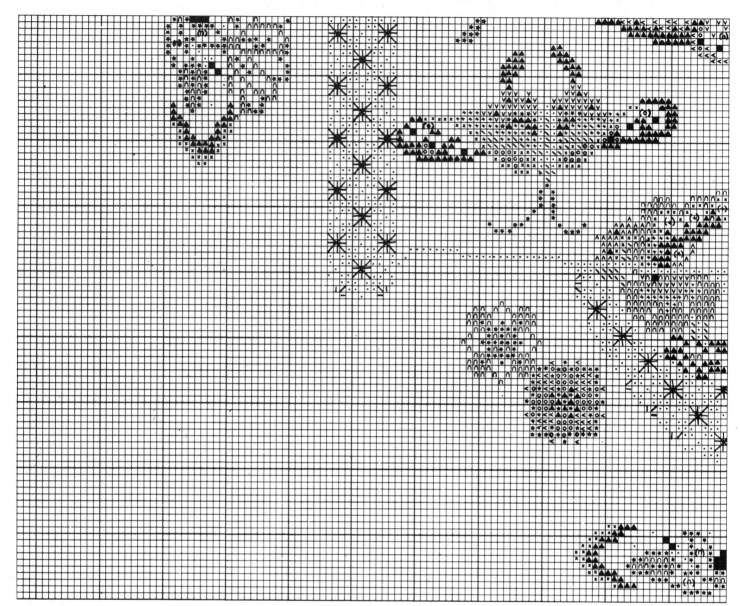

Butterfly Scroll Plate: Lower left

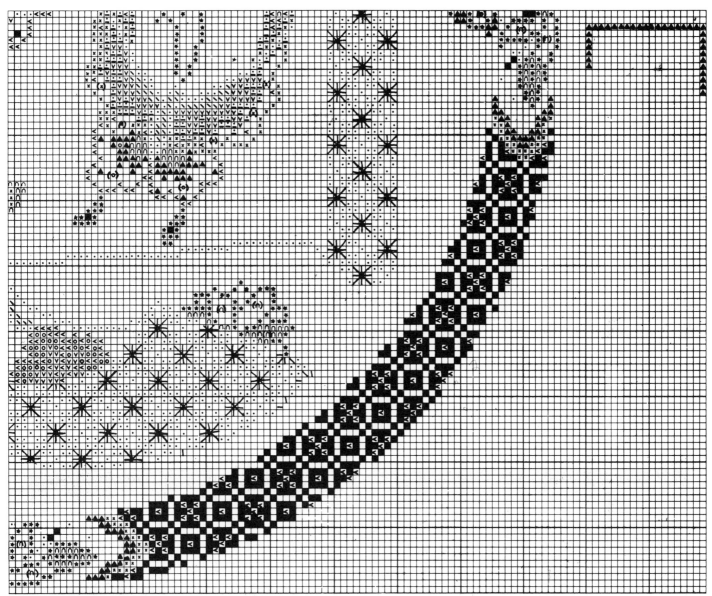

Butterfly Scroll Plate: Lower right

🦢 Malay Peacock Pillow

The peacock of the "Mandarin Square" is the rank insignia of a third-degree civil official. Mandarin Squares were worn on the outer coats by nobles, civil officials, and the military to denote rank. Various birds designated the nine official civil ranks, and nine various animals designated the military. The upper ranks were assigned the more dignified and stately birds; the lower, the lesser.

The peacock is believed to have been introduced to China from the Malay Peninsula. Highly prized, its feathers were awarded for meritorious and faithful service. As an emblem of beauty, splendor, and dignity, the peacock is an important part of the universe. Here, the universe is represented by the clouds of heaven over the waves, with the rocks and mountains denoting Earth and its permanence. The covered vase in the waves is the Store of Truth and conveys the wish for "peace, tranquillity, and knowledge." Prosperity, imparted by the precious jewels floating amid the waves, is part of the overall wish for "Peace, Knowledge, and Continued Success for a long time to come."

	Malay Peacock Pillow	DMC Colors
o	Light Blue	775
I	Blue	931
×	Dark Blue	311
U	Light Coral	352
△	Coral	350
▲	Red	347
∴	White	—
v	Yellow	725
▪	Golden Brown	781
-	Light Green	504
+	Green	502
●	Dark Green	895
<	Gold Metallic	—

Stitch Count: 165 by 165

Malay Peacock Pillow

Malay Peacock: Right half

Malay Peacock: Left half

᷎᷒Lotus and Kingfisher Panel

The original embroidery from which this panel is adapted, entitled *Kingfisher and Lotus Flower*, is the tenth leaf from the Album "Everlasting Verdure of Elysian Parks." The album is a part of the textile collection of the National Palace Museum in Taipei, Taiwan, and is from the Ch'ing dynasty (1644–1911.) The album is a series of embroideries praising such simple subjects as the kingfisher, the lotus, butterflies, and other flowers. The original is worked in satin stitch on a woven silk twill fabric; the entire background was painted blue after the embroidery was completed.

The lotus flower, which remains untainted even as it struggles and grows out of the mud of the swamp, is emblematic of the completeness of a wise man's virtue. The kingfisher's magnificent blue-green plumage represents the nuances of beauty.

This piece can be appreciated simply as a decorative piece depicting a brilliant summer's day (the lotus is a symbol of summer) with the lotus in full bloom and the beautiful but vain kingfisher admiring his reflection in the pond.

The diaper pattern (a repetitive pattern covering an entire area) above and below the piece implies the wish for a "myriad of happiness and prosperity in the attainment of old age" through the use of the interlocking fylfot *wan*, the *shou*, and the coin motifs. *Note* that the patterns that follow show only the upper diaper pattern. Repeat the pattern in reverse for the lower portion.

Lotus and Kingfisher Panel		DMC Colors
⊂	White	—
\	Ecru	—
•	Beige	644
▲	Dark Beige	642
⊀	Light Brown	422
▰	Dark Brown	610
o	Light Green	504
†	Medium Green	320
△	Dark Green	319
✶	Black Green	991
×	Aqua	598
∩	Peacock Blue	806
∨	Light Coral	353
–	Dark Coral	351
◆	Black	310
	Yellow	745
⁄	Dark Blue	312

Stitch Count (entire piece with diaper pattern): 167 by 364
Stitch Count (design area only): 167 by 186

Lotus and Kingfisher:
Upper third

Lotus and Kingfisher:
Middle third

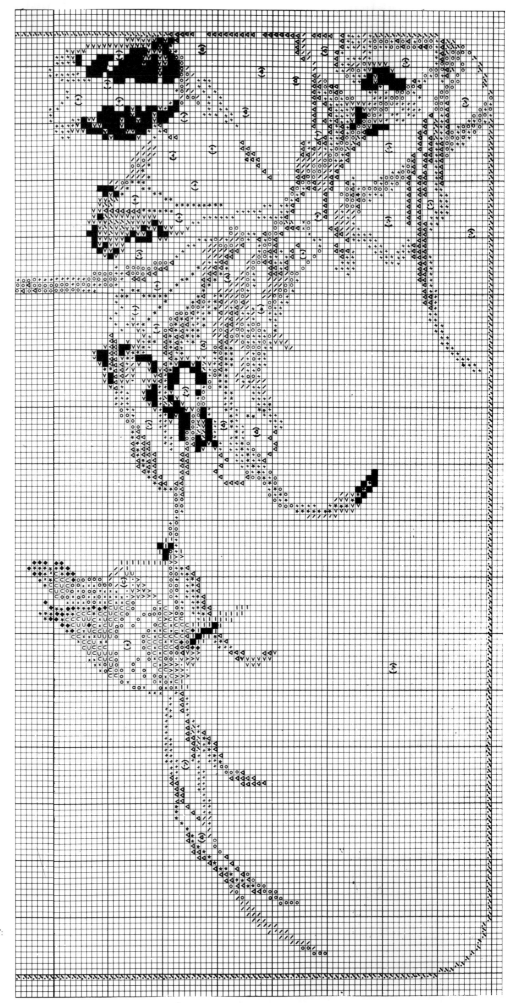

Lotus and Kingfisher:
Lower third

Ming Basket Cushion

The original piece is a woodblock color print made in the early seventeenth century (Ming dynasty, 1368–1644) and is part of the collection at the British Museum in London.

The Hundred Antiquities are numerous items (hundred being used to imply many, not literally one hundred) from ink pots to musical instruments, from sacrificial vessels to writing implements, that are emblematic of cultural refinement. Of these, a favored design motif is the flower basket. It was said to be carried by those fairies who were the benefactors of mankind and was believed to possess supernatural powers through the flowers' blossoms.

In addition to the intrinsic attributes, the basket incorporates the interlocking circle pattern called the "Golden Coin" design. This same pattern forms the border and conveys the wish for "prosperity and riches." The coin, one of the Eight Precious Things (symbols of culture) from the Hundred Antiquities, also represents completeness in the harmonious balance between heaven and earth.

The "cloud-collar" band above the coin design on the basket is adapted from the form of the sacred fungus and expresses the hope that "all one's hopes and desires will be fulfilled." The wish is accompanied by the implication of power and good fortune.

The peony, called the "queen of flowers," is held in highest esteem and has many meanings attached to it—love, feminine beauty, honors, and wealth, to name but a few. Its blooms imply a lush beauty with a definite romantic allure. The peach blossom is another spring flower and is imbued with the qualities of youth and freshness. It is an emblem of spring, marriage, and fruitfulness.

The flower basket is filled with peony, peach blossom, and lily (symbol of maternity and of creative power) and so is a statement of love, beauty, and the fulfillment of dreams. This basket might have been given, with great affection, to a young lady by her beau.

Note: Only part of the border, which should extend all the way around the cushion, is shown in the following patterns. Continue border all the way around cushion in same pattern (see photo in color section for complete border).

Ming Basket Cushion		DMC Colors
✕	Dark Blue	797
o	Blue	809
✓	Light Green	504
+	Medium Green	993
▪	Dark Green	991
⊂	Light Rose	819
△	Medium Rose	223
•	Red	326
>	Light Yellow	745
\	Medium Yellow	725
▲	Brown	300

Stitch Count (entire piece): 233 by 197

Butterfly Pillow

The "stemless flower," which is what Chinese artists sometimes call the butterfly, universally evokes emotions of delight and joy and images of the beauty of free flight, sunshine, and beautiful flowers. The tips of this butterfly's wings are decorated with a pattern of peacock feathers. These emblems augment the butterfly's beauty and impart added dignity.

The central design motif on the wings is a cluster of lichee nuts. The lichee was not indigenous to China and was, therefore, considered to be exotic and extravagant. As a symbol, it is not as rich in associations as are many others. However, it is considered to be of good taste, exotic, colorful, and romantically charming.

Butterfly Pillow		DMC Colors
✬	Light Green	369
<	Medium Green	320
•	Dark Green	319
-	Beige	822
∧	Light Brown	642
+	Medium Brown	841
▲	Dark Brown	839
o	Light Yellow	3047
∆	Dark Yellow	3045
×	Dark Yellow Brown	420
∪	Light Plum	3042
◪	Dark Plum	3041
⟍	Gold Metallic	—

Stitch Count: 229 by 172

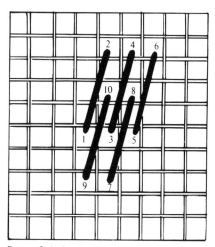

Butterfly's body

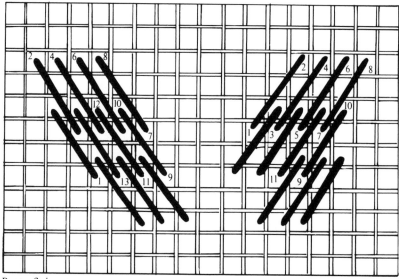

Butterfly's wings

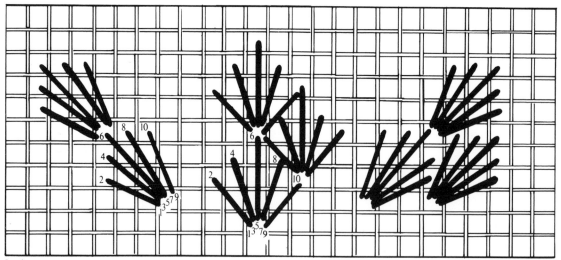

Lichee nuts

Butterfly Pillow

Butterfly: Upper left

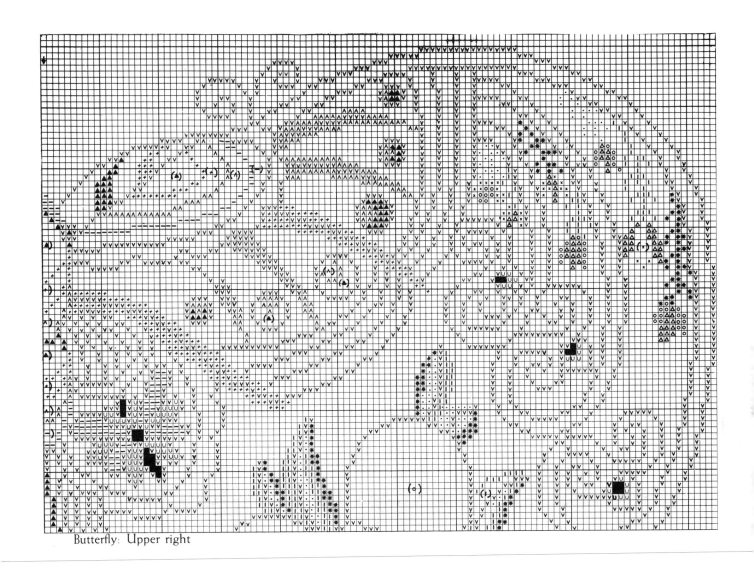

Butterfly: Upper right

Butterfly: Lower left

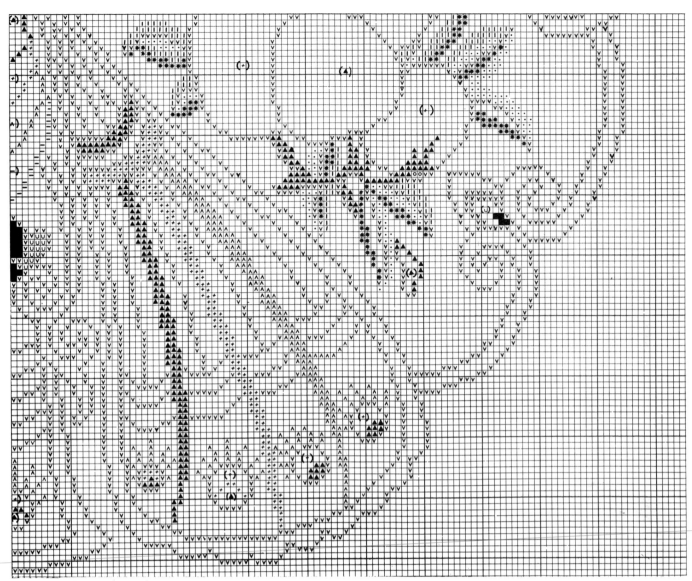

Butterfly: Lower right

Tiger Lilies Pillow

The tiger lilies, with lovely bamboo set in the rocks (symbolizing earth, permanence, and solidarity), are a simple statement of faith, courage, graceful continuity, permanence, and perpetuity.

The bamboo is called the "friend of China" and is appreciated for its beauty, its symbolism, and its inherent attributes as well as its practicality. It denotes endurance, flexibility, and dependability, since it bends in the face of a storm but does not break. Its hollow stem holds truth and reason; and, as it flourishes throughout the year, it typifies courage, faithfulness, and virtue. The graceful and beautiful images and symbolism of the bamboo are furthered by the tiger lilies as an emblem of maternity and creative power—of perpetuity—nurtured by the elements of the earth.

Tiger Lilies Pillow		DMC Colors
o	Light Green	3348
✗	Medium Green	320
▲	Dark Green	500
A	Dark Blue	930
∩	Light Blue	932
•	Dark Rust	919
+	Light Rust	921
‹	Dark Yellow	729
＼	Light Yellow	677

Stitch Count: 123 by 123

Tiger Lilies Pillow

✍️ Manchurian Crane Pillow

The Manchurian crane, a white bird with a red tuft on top of its head, is the messenger of the gods and is credited with living one thousand years. This crane is adapted from the central medallion of a late-eighteenth-century insignia medallion of the Ch'ing dynasty.

The clouds symbolize heaven and its bounty; the peach branch is a symbol of longevity. As the crane carries the peach branch on its flight through the clouds, it communicates the wish for "mortal success and a long and fruitful life."

Manchurian Crane Pillow		DMC Colors
O	White	—
●	Silver Metallic	—
/	Medium Blue	322
◭	Light Blue	775
<	Dark Blue	336
▲	Beige	945
✕	Coral	352
◆	Green	320
∩	Red	350
✛	Brown	435

Stitch Count: 87 by 84

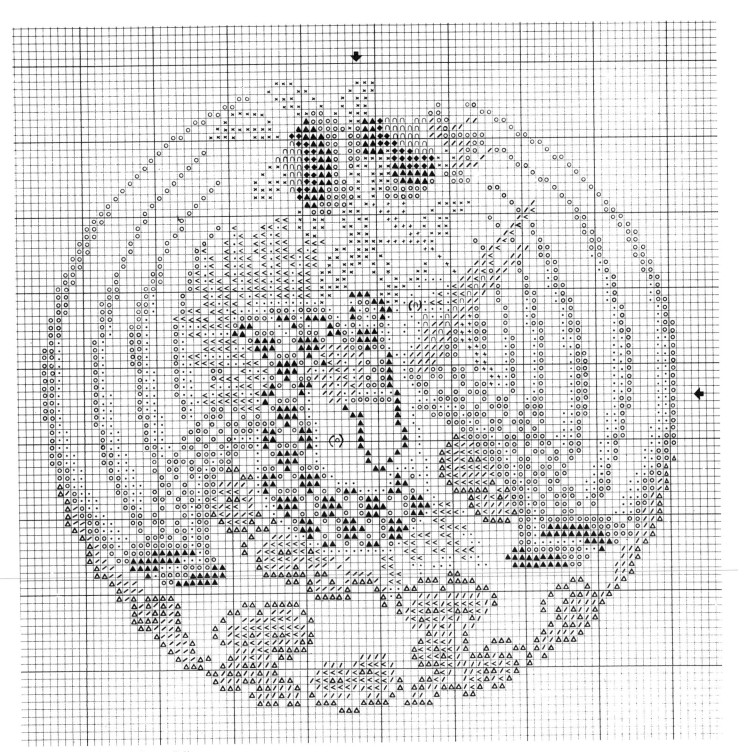

Manchurian Crane Pillow

৯হ Happy Augury Framed Picture Set

The Happy Augury symbols, or "Lucky Emblems of Buddhism," are eight auspicious signs found on the sole of Buddha's foot. The use of the symbols carries a general wish of "luck," with a specific symbolic wish inherent in each different one. The Wheel of Life and the Vase are two of the eight symbols of Happy Augury that are often used with the *shou*, one of the oldest symbols of happiness.

The floating ribbons surrounding each of the motifs are used to set them apart and emphasize their sacred and supernatural powers. The bat, *fu*, is a homonym for the character *fu*, which means "happiness, luck, and good fortune." It is an ancient emblem, revered as the cultivator of divine blessings. When several are used together, as in this border, they impart the wish that one's "long life and happiness be as great as heaven is high."

The Wheel of the Law, or of Life, is an emblem of truth and of heavenly resources. The covered Sacred Vase is a symbol for the Store of Truth and thereby ensures long-lasting peace and harmony.

Wheel of Life

		DMC Colors
✕	Dark Blue	311
•	Medium Blue	931
o	Light Blue	3325
∸	Red	347
▲	Dark Rust	921
+	Light Rust	402
⌐	Yellow	744
Δ	Light Green	504
I	Gold Metallic	—

Stitch Count: 65 by 65

Vase

		DMC Colors
✕	Dark Blue	311
•	Medium Blue	931
o	Light Blue	3325
∸	Red	347
▲	Dark Rust	921
U	Light Rust	402
⌐	Yellow	744
†	Dark Green	912
I	Gold Metallic	—

Stitch Count: 65 by 65

Yellow *Shou*

		DMC Colors
Δ	Blue	311
•	Medium Blue	931
o	Light Blue	3325
⁄	Red	347
▲	Dark Rust	921
✕	Dark Yellow	783
<	Yellow	676
I	Gold Metallic	—

Red *Shou*

Δ	Blue	311
•	Medium Blue	391
o	Light Blue	3325
⁄	Dark Yellow	783
◢	Yellow	676
✕	Dark Rust	921
<	Red	347
I	Gold Metallic	—

Stitch Count: 65 by 65

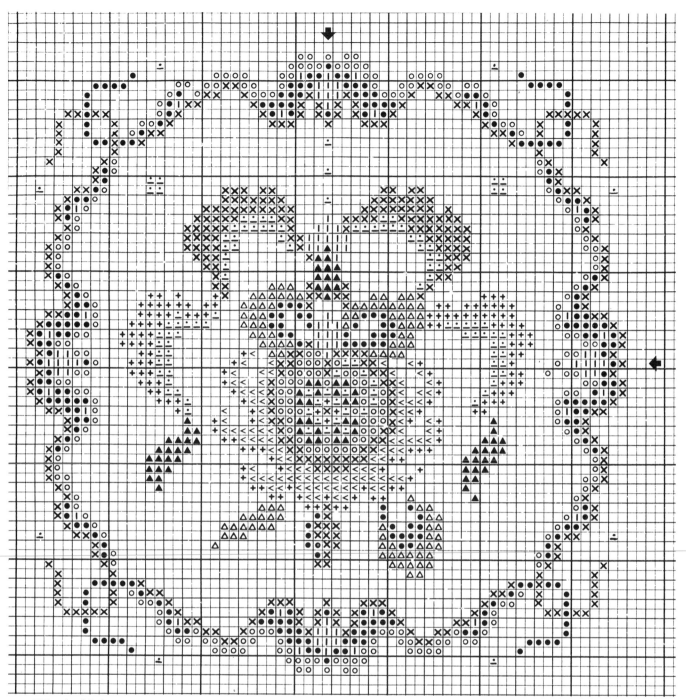

Wheel of Life

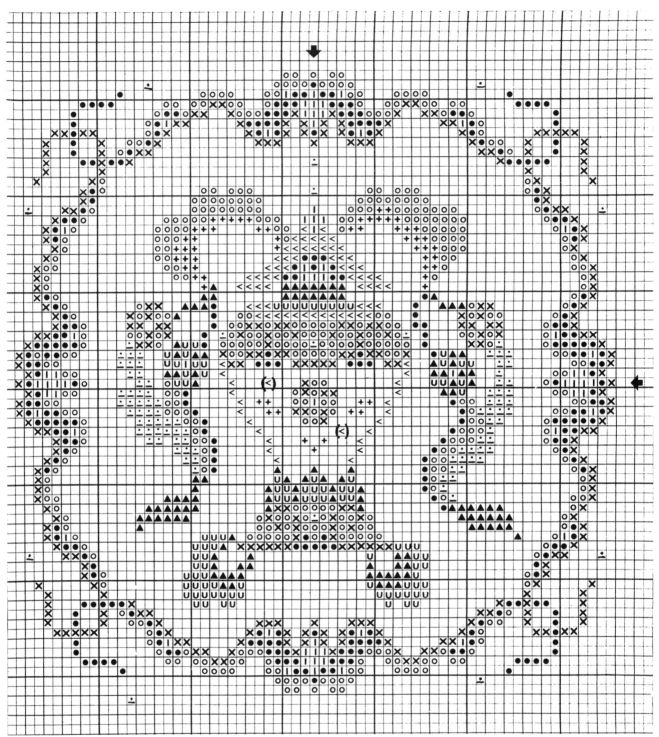

Vase

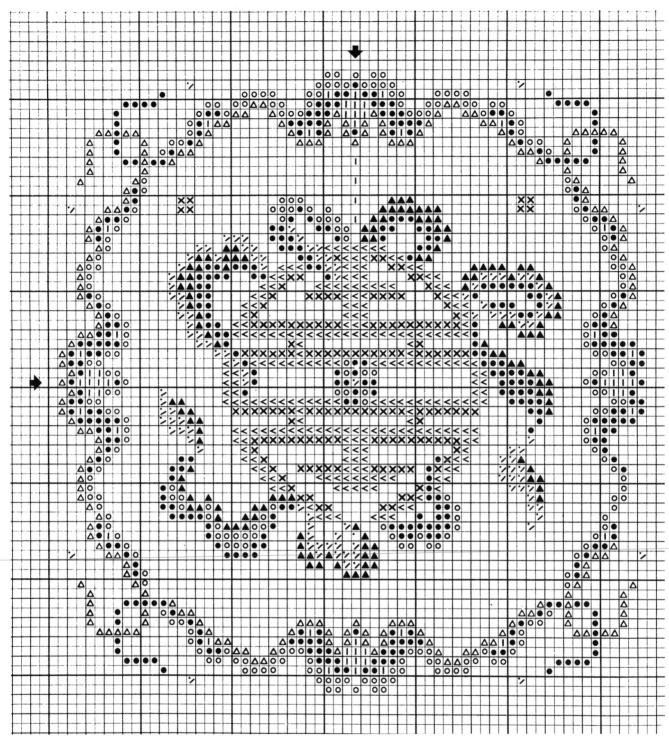

Shou

﹖Pomegranate and Butterfly Framed Picture

These two design elements were often used together on items given as wedding gifts. The pomegranate is the symbol of fertility, and the butterfly is a rebus for felicity and happiness.

	Pomegranate and Butterfly Framed Picture	DMC Colors
o	Light Blue	813
✶	Dark Blue	823
◢	Dark Green	911
×	Light Green	955
△	Gray	415
+	Red	349
＼	Light Yellow	744
•	Gold	783
∧	Rust	921

Stitch Count: 67 by 67

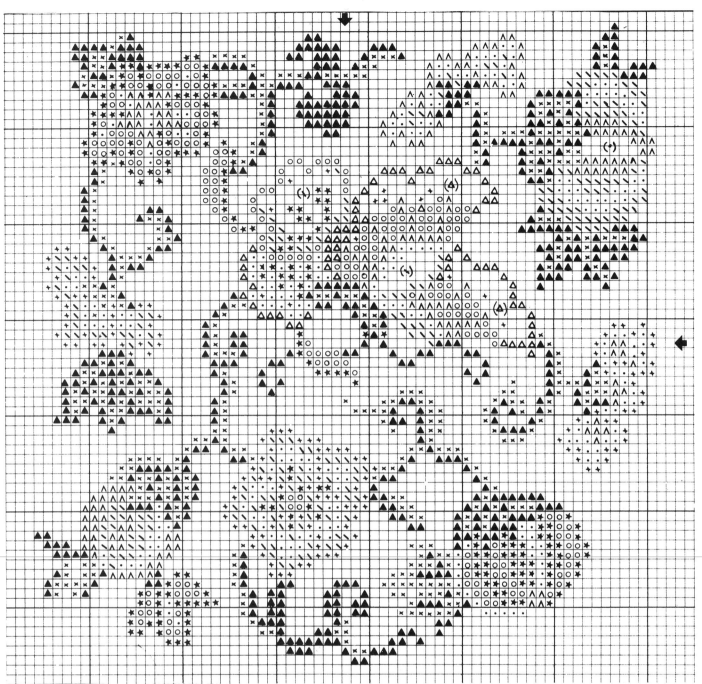

Pomegranate and Butterfly Framed Picture

Additional Designs

  The following four designs (Goldfish Medallion, Butterfly Medallion, Chrysanthemums, and Basket of Prosperity) are small motifs that could be used to create or embellish a lovely sachet, a pincushion, a corner for a placemat and napkins, a border for hand towels, or a table runner. They may also be expanded into larger projects (such as pillows or hangings) by repeating a motif several times, using two of them alternately in a row, or by using diaper patterns and borders to create whatever size or project one chooses.

  The color key accompanying each piece is only a suggested one. The color choices available to the needleworker in cottons, silks, and wools are almost as limitless as the projects and combinations one can imagine.

Goldfish Medallion		DMC Colors
∩	Black or Dark Blue	824
▲	Blue	519
•	Gold	972

Stitch Count: 79 by 75

Butterfly Medallion		DMC Colors
▲	Pale Celadon Green	504
o	Soft Yellow or Soft Peach	727
•	Medium Blue	826

Stitch Count: 79 by 79

Chrysanthemums		DMC Colors
▰	Dark Green	991
△	Light Green	320
✕	Dark Blue	312
▲	Rust	921
•	Light Rust	402

Stitch Count: 76 by 69

Basket of Prosperity		DMC Colors
•	Yellow	744
▲	Brown	839
✕	Blue	798
■	Blue Green	992
+	Coral	356
∨	Light Coral	758
o	Light Brown	842
∪	Light Green	504
∆	Medium Green	502
	Dark Green (Backstitch)	500
⸜	Black	310

Stitch Count: 76 by 60

Chrysanthemums

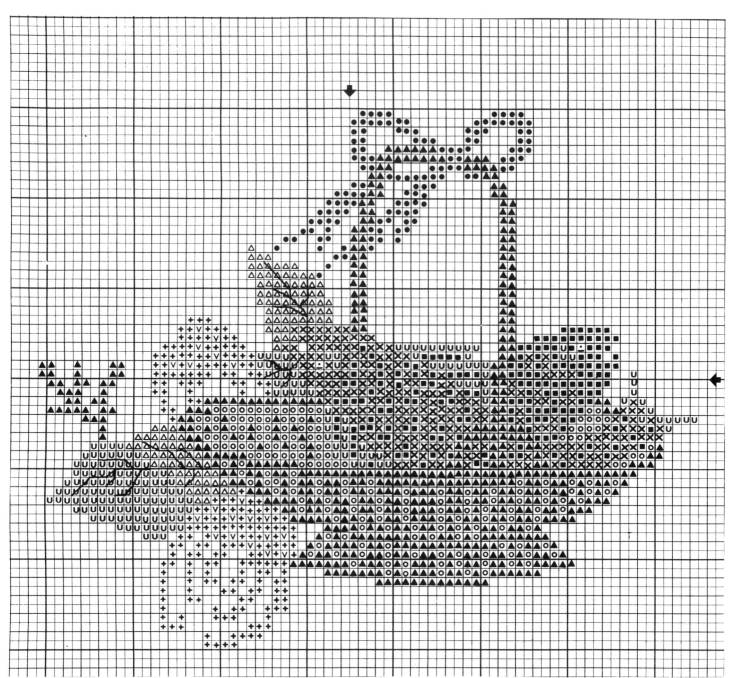

Basket of Prosperity

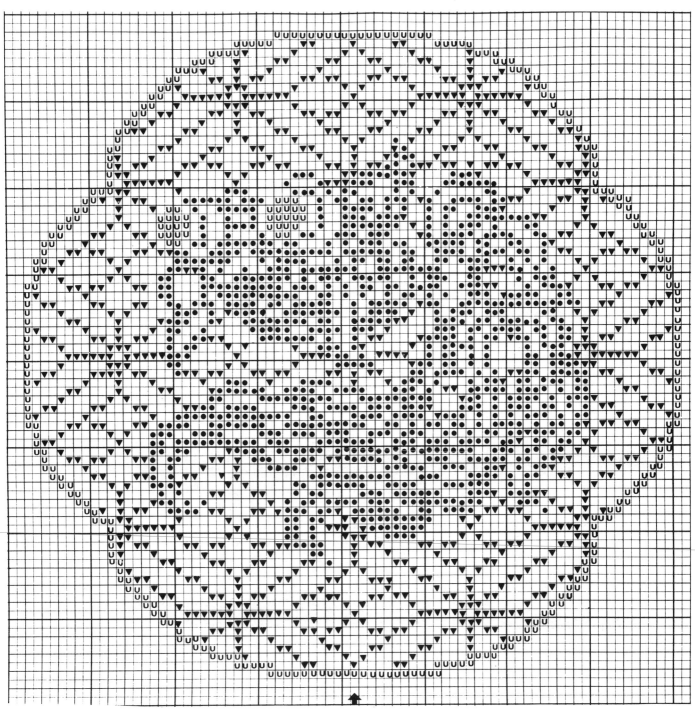

Goldfish Medallion

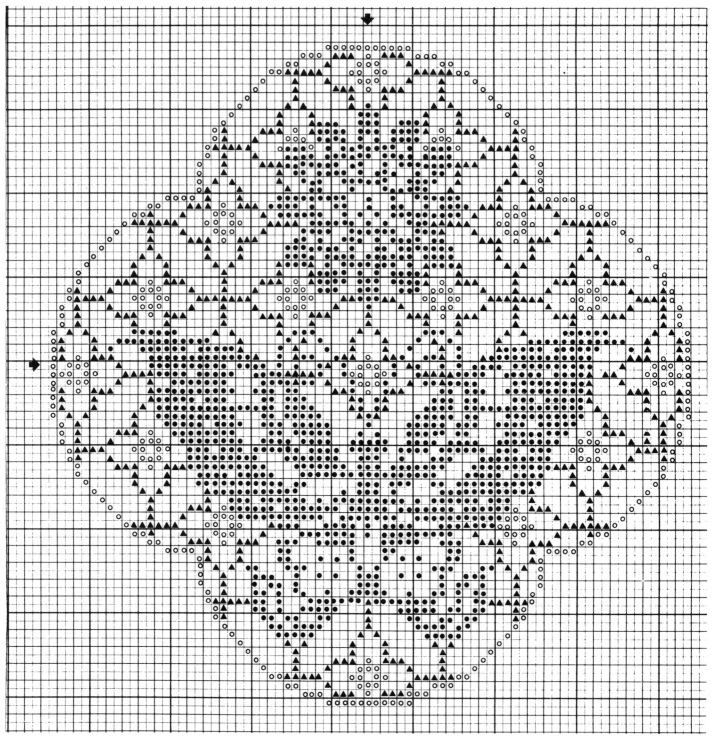

Butterfly Medallion

Borders, Corners, and Diaper Patterns

Border patterns (those motifs used on the edges of a design or surrounding a design), diaper patterns (those motifs that form an "all-over" background pattern), and corner patterns (usually the corner for a border pattern) are used consistently throughout Chinese art. Their symmetry, which often incorporates various symbols, contributes to the overall effect. Many border patterns are interchangeable. You might also add a border, or even two, to a small piece to make it larger. Use borders and diaper patterns (changing colors, if you wish) to create an entirely different effect or project.

Borders and Corners

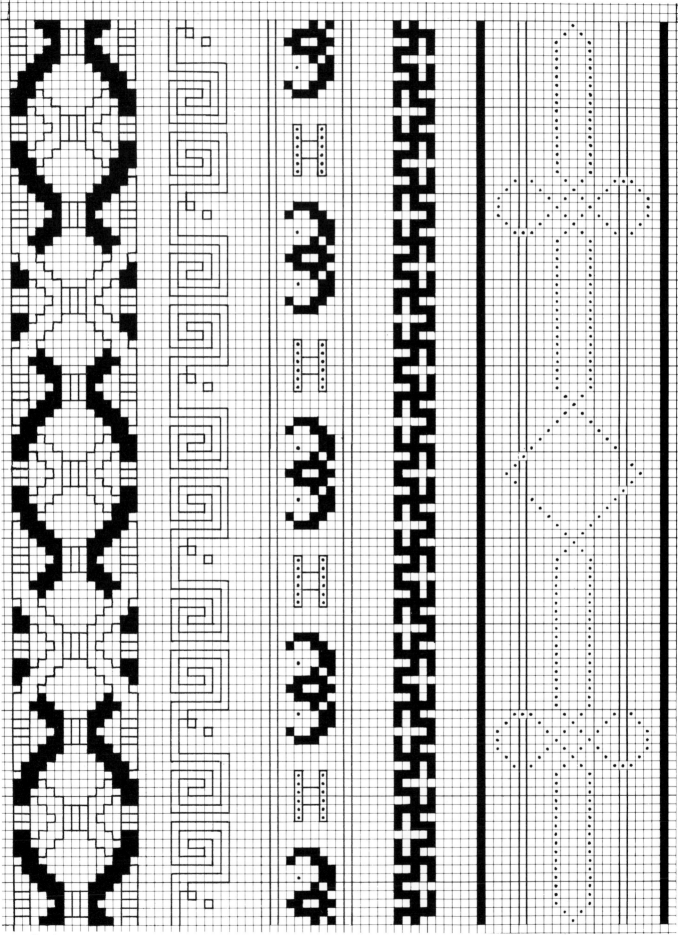

Borders

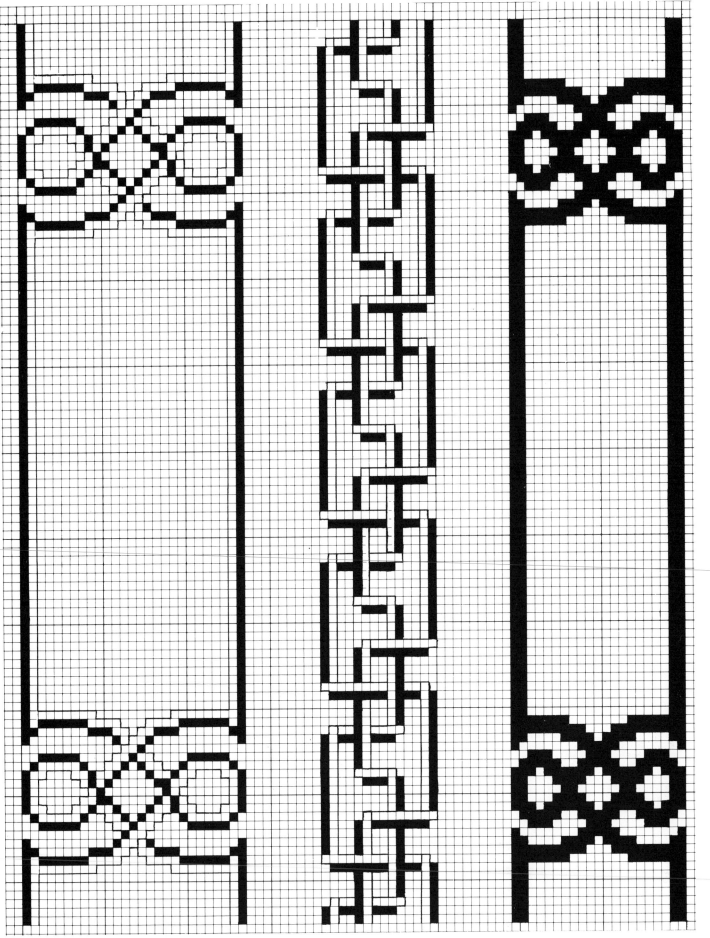

Borders

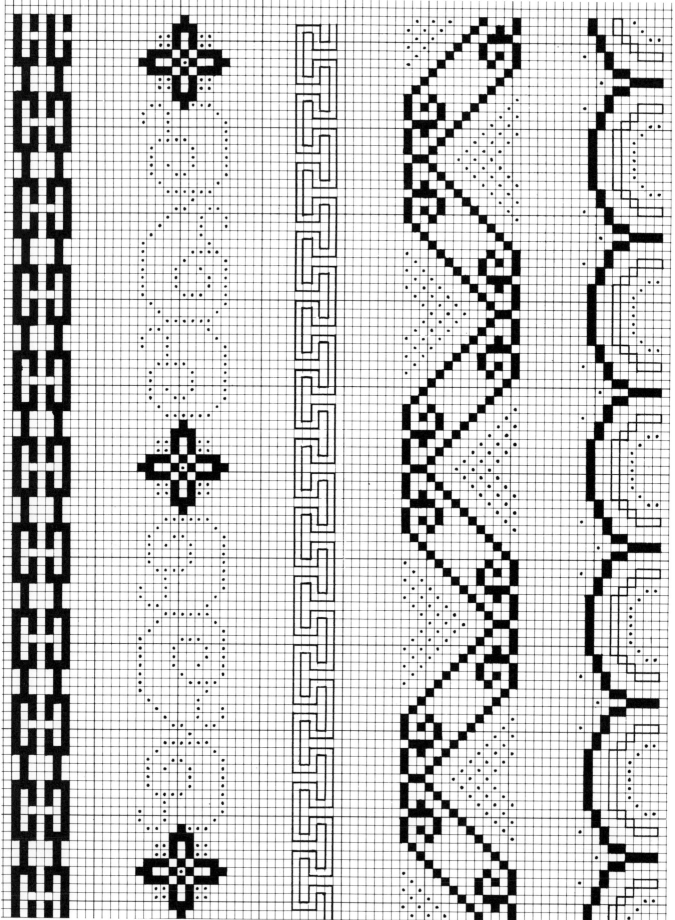

Borders

Borders

Diaper Patterns

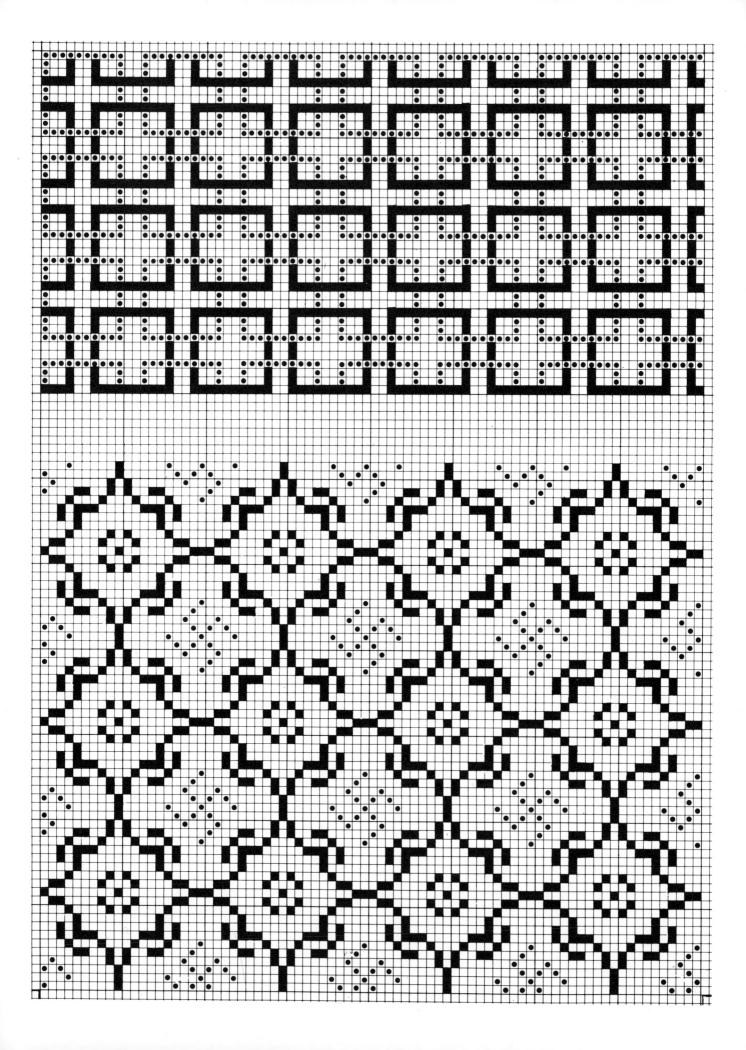

Notes on the Color Photographs

Lotus and Kingfisher Panel
Stitched by Jane Ofstrom. Needlepoint on 18-mesh canvas.
Finished size: stitched area—9 by 20 inches
(22.5 by 50 cm)
inside frame—13.5 by 24 inches
(33.75 by 60 cm)

Butterfly Scroll (left)
Stitched by Carlene Stotler. Cross-stitch on 18-count Davos.
Finished size: stitched area—12 by 12 inches
(30 by 30 cm)
pillow—12.75 by 12.75 inches
(32 by 32 cm)

Spring Vase (right)
Stitched by Kathy McDonald. Cross-stitch on 18-count Davos.
Finished size: 10.25 by 15 inches
(25.5 by 37.5 cm)

Malay Peacock Pillow
Stitched by Carlene Stotler. Cross-stitch on 14-count yellow Aida.
Finished size: stitched area—12 by 12 inches
(30 by 30 cm)
pillow—12.5 by 12.5 inches
(31.25 by 31.25 cm)

Tiger Lilies Pillow (left)
Stitched by Mary Alleyne. Cross-stitch on 27-count Linda over two threads.
Finished size: stitched area—9.5 by 9.5 inches
(23.75 by 23.75 cm)
pillow—10.5 by 10.5 inches
(26.25 by 26.25 cm)

Butterfly Pillow (right)
Stitched by Inch Sharp. Needlepoint on 18-mesh canvas.
Finished size: 13.25 by 9.5 inches
(33 by 23.75 cm)

Center front: Original "Butterfly," embroidered with silk threads and gold couching on silk. (Courtesy of the Vallin Gallery)

Dragon-Fish Screen (top right)
Stitched by Lisa Lloyd. Cross-stitch on 18-count Davos.
Finished size: Stitched area of each panel—
4.5 by 9.75 inches
(11.25 by 24.25 cm)
opening of each panel—
4.5 by 11.5 inches
(11.25 by 28.75 cm)
(Two-panel miniscreen courtesy of Sudberry House)

Pomegranate and Butterfly Framed Picture (lower right)
Stitched by Julia Alleyne. Cross-stitch on 22-count Hardanger.
Finished size: 3.5 by 3.5 inches
      (8.75 by 8.75 cm)

Happy Augury Picture Set (left and center front)
From top to bottom: *The Wheel, the Yellow Shou, the Vase,* and *the Red Shou.* Each cross-stitched on 22-count Hardanger.
Finished size: 3.5 by 3.5 inches
      (8.75 by 8.75 cm)

Ming Bird Panel
Stitched by Mary Alleyne and Marion Scolar. Cross-stitch on 25-count Blue Dublin linen over two threads.
Finished size: stitched area—16.25 by 38 inches
      (40.5 by 95 cm)

Narcissus and Shou Rug
Stitched by MICHIKO of Haiti. Needlepoint on 8-mesh canvas.
Finished size: 53.5 by 78.5 inches
      (133.75 by 196.25 cm)

Narcissus and Shou Rug (background)
Spring Vase Hanging
Stitched by Carlene Stotler. Cross-stitch on 22-count Hardanger.
Finished size: 8.25 by 12.25 inches
      (20.5 by 30.5 cm)
(Antique frame courtesy of Vallin Gallery)

Narcissus and Hsi Evening Clutch
Stitched on 18-mesh canvas by MICHIKO of Haiti.
Finished size (closed): 7.5 by 5 inches
      (18.75 by 12.5 cm)

Manchurian Crane Pillow
Stitched by Linda Herring. Cross-stitch on 22-count dark blue Hardanger.
Finished size: diameter of stitched area—3.5
      inches (8.75 cm)
      finished diameter—4.25 inches
      (10.5 cm)

Ming Basket Cushion
Stitched by Linda Herring. Cross-stitch on 14-count cream Gardasee.
Finished size: 17 by 14.5 inches
      (42.5 by 36.25 cm)
(Chinese Chippendale bench courtesy of Plain 'N Fancy)

Bibliography

Alexander, Mary, and Frances Alexander. *A Handbook on Chinese Art Symbols*. Austin, Texas: Von Boeckmann-Jones, 1972.

Auboyer, Jeannine, and Roger Goepper. *The Oriental World*. Landmarks of the World's Art Series. New York: McGraw-Hill, 1967.

Ayers, John. *The Baur Collection, Geneva. Chinese Ceramics*, Vol. 4. Geneva: Collections Baur, 1974.

Ball, Katherine M. *Decorative Motives of Oriental Art*. New York: Hacker Art Books, 1969.

Burling, Judith, and Arthur H. Burling. *Chinese Art*. New York: Thomas Y. Crowell and Studio Publications, 1953.

Chavannes, Eduoard. *The Five Happinesses: Symbolism in Chinese Popular Art*. Translated by Elaine S. Atwood. New York: Weatherhill, 1973.

Christie, Anthony. *Chinese Mythology*. Middlesex, England: Hamlyn Publishing Group, 1968.

Coen, Luciano, and Louise Duncan. *The Oriental Rug*. New York: Harper & Row, 1978.

Dimand, M. S. *Oriental Rugs in the Metropolitan Museum of Art*. New York: New York Graphic Society and Metropolitan Museum of Art, 1973.

du Boulay, Anthony. *Chinese Porcelain*. London: Octopus Books, 1963.

Fernald, Helen E. *Chinese Court Costumes*. Toronto: Royal Ontario Museum of Archaeology, 1946.

Fong, Wen. *The Great Bronze Age of China*. New York: Alfred A. Knopf and Metropolitan Museum of Art, 1980.

Gostelow, Mary. *The Cross-Stitch Book*. New York: Van Nostrand Reinhold Company Inc., 1982.

Hackmack, Adolf. *Chinese Carpets and Rugs*. Translated by L. Arnold. New York: Dover, 1973.

Hay, John. *Masterpieces of Chinese Art*. Greenwich: New York Graphic Society, 1974.

Keswick, Maggie. *The Chinese Garden: History, Art and Architecture*. New York: Rizzoli, 1978.

Le Corbeiller, Claire. *China Trade Porcelain: Patterns of Exchange*. New York: New York Graphic Society and Metropolitan Museum of Art, 1974.

Lorentz, H. A. *A View of Chinese Rugs from the Seventeenth to the Twentieth Century*. London: Routledge & Kegan Paul, 1972.

Mailey, Jean. *Chinese Silk and Tapestry: K'o-ssu*. New York: China Institute in America, 1971.

Mailey, Jean. *Embroidery of Imperial China*. New York: China Institute in America, 1978.

Masterpieces of Chinese Silk Tapestry and Embroidery in the National Palace Museum. Taipei, Taiwan: National Palace Museum, 1971.

Nott, Stanley C. *Voices from the Flowery Kingdom*. New York: Chinese Culture Study Group of America, 1947.

Peterson, Grete, and Svennas, Elsie. *Handbook of Stitches*. New York: Van Nostrand Reinhold Company, 1970.

Priest, Alan. *Aspects of Chinese Painting*. New York: Macmillan, 1954.

——— *Costumes from the Forbidden City*. New York: Metropolitan Museum of Art, 1945.

Pruitt, Ida, ed. *The Flight of an Empress: Told by Wu Yung Whose Other Name is Yü-ch'uan.* Transcribed by Liu K'un. New Haven, Conn.: Yale University Press, 1936.

Ridley, Michael. *Style Motif and Design in Chinese art.* Dorset, England: Blandford Press, 1977.
——— *Treasures of China.* New York: Arco, 1973.

Simmons, Pauline. *Chinese Patterned Silks.* New York: Metropolitan Museum of Art, 1948.

Sowerby, Arthur deC. *Nature in Chinese Art.* New York: John Day, 1940.

Tiffany Studios. *Antique Chinese Rugs.* Rutland, Vt.: Charles E. Tuttle, 1969.

Trubner, Henry, et al., eds. *Asiatic Art in the Seattle Art Museum.* Seattle, Wash.: Seattle Art Museum, 1973.

Vollmer, John E. *In the Presence of the Dragon Throne.* Toronto: Royal Ontario Museum, 1977.

Williams, C. A. S. *Outline of Chinese Symbolism and Art Motives.* 3rd rev. ed. Rutland, Vt.: Charles E. Tuttle, 1974.

Wright-Smith, Rosamund. *Picture Framing.* New York: Van Nostrand Reinhold Company Inc., 1982.

Index